John Carr of York

Architect

1723 - 1807

Preface

My first sight of Tabley House, designed by John Carr, took place during the winter of 1945-6, when Germany had been defeated, but before the end of the war against Japan, a time when no lights were permitted anywhere outside. I was thirteen at the time. One of the consequences was that I missed the bus that should have taken me the six or so miles from Tabley to Altrincham, and from there via another bus, to nearer home in outer Manchester. The six-mile walk in the dark, on the verge of a main road, was highly unpleasant, and since we had no telephone, I could not phone home. Since then, I have seen virtually every standing building designed by John Carr, and none has failed to give me a degree of pleasure.

My next foray was to Harewood House, then newly coming out of its wartime requisitioning to resume its earlier function as the country home of the Princess Royal. My mentor then was Mr Ernest Hollowell, Art Master at Manchester Grammar School who gave me every encouragement and, in particular, that insight into architecture, books and photography, out of which this book has evolved. Thereafter I travelled as far as my bike would take me until, from the early 1960s onward, I travelled in greater comfort in the car of Dr Gordon Drummond who was to become a faithful and lifelong friend. Together (and with my son John) we went to Oporto to see Carr's great, if sadly incomplete, hospital. The only thing Gordon and I did not visit together was Coolattin in Ireland.

Without these many years of generosity, by Gordon and many others, family or friends, what follows in this book would not have been possible. A new lease of life came when I acquired the digital cameras that allowed a fuller pictorial coverage than had been possible hitherto, and for this renaissance John must be given the credit. (I have not always been a good pupil.) More recently still I have had the most generous help from Mr Danial Foster who takes me where I need to go, and takes photographs at sites which I can no longer reach. Fortunately he is blessed with a good eye for a composition. Many thanks to Rachel Hall, William Carver, Margaret Carver and Willa McDonald for proofreading and editing. Finally to revert to John Hall: this book was suggested by him, and pushed forward to a successful conclusion by him.

This book is dedicated to the memory of Elisabeth A. F. Hall (1932-1995).

Dr Ivan Hall

Acknowledgements

I am grateful to the British Academy and the York Georgian Society for their grants in aid of my research. Thanks are also due to the following who gave permission for the publication of various photographs: Father Brian Bell; Mr P. Bell; the Director of Bootham Park Hospital; Mr Mark Broadwith; Mr Karl Brown; Mr C.D. Carr; Mr Robin Compton; Mr Roger Dyson; Mr J. Etherington; Mr Danial Foster; Mr Philip Guest; The Earl and Countess of Harewood and the Trustees of Harewood House Trust; Harrogate Borough Council; Mr Jason Hawkes; the Honourable Simon Howard; Mr Richard Marriott; Messrs J.H. McCloy and Co. Ltd.; the National Portrait Gallery; the National Trust; Patty Temple of Newark Town Council; Norton Hall Stables Management Company; Plompton High Grange Farm; Rotherham District Council; the Chief Executive, Santo Antonio Hospital, Oporto; Rev. Graham Shield; Mr Christopher Turczak; Mr M.W. Webster; Mr M. C. Wyvill; York Civic Trust; the Dean and Chapter of York Minster.

Printed by GKD Litho Limited, Origination House, 15 Strawberry Street, Hull, HU9 1EZ http://www.gkd-litho.com

Published by Rickaro Books

Table of Contents

Carr's Place in the Profession.

Carr was born at Horbury in 1723, within the parish of Wakefield, County Town of the (former) West Riding of Yorkshire. He probably attended Wakefield Grammar School prior to his training under his father, Robert, who was one of a long line of stonemasons and building contractors, and ambitious enough to tackle architectural projects in the vicinity. In 1743 Robert became one of the joint County Surveyors. This gave him frequent and regular contact with the county's Magistrates, all of whom were at the very least well-to-do gentlemen. Following his father's death in 1760, John Carr succeeded to his father's post.

By that time John had started his own career in York, having decided not to chance his luck in London, but to consolidate an already firm foundation in an area that was becoming increasingly prosperous, was well endowed with potential patrons of wealth and taste, and which was amply served by both skilled craftsmen and excellent building materials. He sensed that the spirit of building was in the air, and that by dint of his own hard work there was money to be made. Politically he was an ardent Whig, as were many of his potential patrons, and the latter's friends and relations added to the web of patronage. He early recognised that he would have to learn the arts of diplomacy in a world of cut-throat competition, especially from young contemporaries only too anxious to brush aside a provincially-based rival. They, unlike Carr, typically had had the benefit of foreign travel, and to make up for this undoubted disadvantage, Carr set about collecting and familiarising himself with a substantial professional working library. Interestingly he was allotted more plates in the successive later volumes of Vitruvius Britannicus than any other architect, and in 1791 was to be invited to join the London Architects Club, a privilege normally reserved for those practising in the capital.

Left: Portrait of John Carr by Sir William Beechey 1791 (National Portrait Gallery).

In the absence of Carr's bank account, neither his income nor his outgoing expenses have proved possible to determine. We know that his earliest professional assistant was William Lindley (1739-1818) who in 1774 advertised an almost thirty year connection with Carr. He was followed by the elder Peter Atkinson (1735-1805), who had obtained some degree of private practice by the later 1790s. It is likely that the younger Peter Atkinson (1780-1843) had at least some links with Carr's practice, especially in connection with later building work on the Harewood Estate. Carr also made a brief reference to his un-named 'ornament man', and to his 'boy'. Given the great extent of his practice this was indeed a modest establishment. Carr's combined house and office was in Skeldergate, York, overlooking a commercial quay-side of the River Ouse. Like many architects he designed his own house, but added an extra doorway to one side as a business entrance, which, with its columns and pediment, was scarcely smaller than the principal entrance nearby.

Unlike Robert Adam, Carr rarely made office copies, so that the surviving drawings typically represent unexecuted schemes, or those that were made just prior to final approval. Once the latter had been given, the contract drawings would be prepared, probably by an assistant.

The client would receive a set of presentation drawings, and a heavily annotated set would go to the selected contractor, who rarely if ever returned them. Finally, Carr would make a set of full-size drawings, in pen or red chalk, so that the craftsmen would know exactly what was required of them.

Once work had started Carr would visit the site to check that the initial setting out had been correctly performed, and then a sequence of visits would be arranged to see both the clients and the selected craftsmen, preferably in a manageable circular tour to avoid wasting either valuable office time or travel time. During Carr's absences from York, an assistant would inform clients that Carr would make contact upon his return. Carr rarely if ever delegated any authority to a junior.

By such means he kept his practice outgoings down to a minimum, while maintaining a full personal and professional responsibility on the other. The latter was not frequent at that time, for many of the most eminent among Carr's London competitors were content to employ 'executive architects' such as William Belwood to do the drudgery for them. The insistence upon a professional responsibility will have endeared Carr to those clients who, while undertaking major works upon their distant estates, yet spent much of their time in London.

Quite apart from the expense of buying, taxing, and maintaining a coach, for most of Carr's working lifetime, many sites were not accessible by coaches, either because the roads were badly maintained, or because the bridges were too narrow to accept the width of a coach. The ideal was to lodge with a client, or to use his house as a base from which to visit others; thereafter it became a matter of staying overnight in an inn, many of which had little to recommend them.

Nearer the end of his life Carr travelled on sightseeing tours with young members of his family and their friends, staying where possible in the homes of one client after another on months' long tours of up to three thousand miles at a time. Here Carr showed his guests not only the standard tourist sights of the time, the rapidly growing cities, and also the interesting workshops and the latest factories then springing up as a part of the Industrial Revolution. In this context, and by any standards, Carr was a modern.

Basildon Park was a new house built of a golden Bath stone for Sir Francis Sykes, a fellow Yorkshireman who had amassed a fortune in India. The site was new and specially selected for its panoramic view northward across the Thames Valley. During the 1760s Carr evolved the simple principle that when the view was exceptional, it should take precedence over architectural display, and conversely the latter should be given to the front facing the duller view. If, as here, wings were needed, they should be sited so as not to interfere with the outward views from the reception rooms, and they should, in themselves, be of visual interest, particularly when seen in perspective. The composition of the entrance front comprises seven parts: each of the three pedimented portions being flanked two minor elements to produce an overall effect of calmness and repose.

Carr's grasp of successfully linking the building to its setting had already be noted by the landscape designer Humphry Repton during Carr's lifetime, and can also be seen in operation at Tabley House and Constable Burton. At the first, the portico projects conventionally forward, but at Constable Burton and Basildon the rear wall was recessed so as to create an indoor/outdoor room or loggia, whose shadow effectively silhouetted the Ionic columns almost regardless of the prevailing weather.

By top lighting the central staircase, Carr avoided corridors, and ensured that no valuable window space was lost on the perimeter. The elegant interior of the house was only partially completed by Carr, who in 1796, stayed with the Sykes family for a week as their guest. Though 'the Roads were bad beyond description for ten miles.....we jaunted about somewhere or other every day....and Lady Sykes took us to Reading fair, where we saw more than ten thousand pounds worth of fine cheese'.

Previous pages: Basildon Park, Berkshire, *(National Trust)*.

Lytham Hall lies on the Lancashire coast to the south of Blackpool. Here Carr incorporated a part of the older house to serve as domestic offices. The cubical villa faces east toward plantations within the park, cut through with rides. The former gate piers, with their iron gates, stood by an existing road and focused the attention upon the house, prior to the creation of a new drive linking the Hall to the railway station. Now it is the end of the house that first comes into view. The commission came just at the changeover from the formal garden with its axial views, to the landscaped garden with its stress upon viewing on the diagonal and an easier link between the house and its garden. There is a local lack of good building materials, but the Lytham elevations are of a strong red brick lavishly dressed with a (now white) painted stone. Though the new landscape style is reflected in the tall ground storey, Carr's Ionic porticoed elevation suggests that there is still a 'piano nobile' (or principal floor) on the floor above. Hence the anomaly of a very grand staircase that leads only to bedrooms. The richly decorated staircase follows the Imperial plan of a central flight to a half landing, then two parallel flights that connect with the main landing. Lytham Hall is notable for the survival of its splendidly carved chimneypieces and doorcases, while the stucco decoration was by the Italian-speaking Swiss, Giuseppe Cortese.

Below: Lytham Hall, chimneypiece.
*Following two pages:*Lytham Hall, facade, and staircase.

Tabley House lies at the edge of the Cheshire plain, a few miles south of Manchester. Carr's patron was an Anglo-Irish baronet Sir Peter Byrne who changed his name to Leicester in 1744. Since the will of his cousin had forbidden the demolition of Tabley (Old) Hall, Sir Peter planned his new house to be on a ridge over-looking Tabley Mere. Carr again chose the sev-en-part composition (see below), also favoured by James Paine, setting the central block boldly forward so that the wings would not interfere with the outward views from the principal re-ception rooms, whilst a great courtyard was extended northward to terminate in a long low block of stables. The initial wish was for a house built entirely of masonry, but the cost of transporting stone of the required quality proved too great, and so, as a compromise, a fine red brick was ordered to be made, but heavily dressed with a red sandstone from the quarries near Runcorn.

Carr did however persuade Sir Peter to pay for four monoliths to be turned into Doric columns for the portico. To avoid prohibitive charges on the turnpike, a special machine was designed to transport the great stones overland, drawn by sixteen horses under the supervision of eight drivers. The lack of colour contrast between the brick and the stone led to the over-painting of all the latter with grey paint. Unusu-ally, a full Doric entablature encircles the building. Interestingly, whereas the standard Doric triglyphs have two channels and two half channels apiece, here there are three full chan-nels. Such unorthodoxy occurs in Leoni's trans-lation of Palladio, and in the (former) eighteenth century Masonic Temple in Great Queen Street, London. According to present day Freemasons, the three channelled triglyph has, however, no special Masonic significance. As at Constable Burton Hall the principal staircase is lit by a Roman style clearstorey. The double curvature of the external staircase gives the portico a continental swagger.

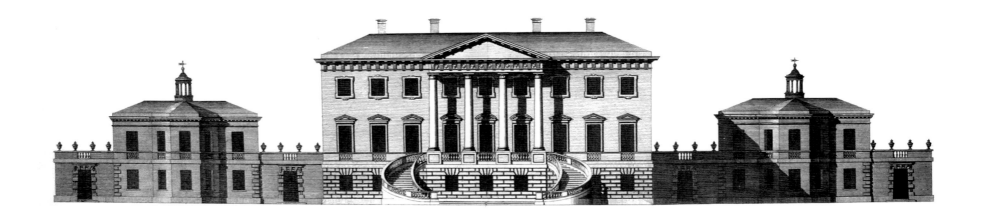

Above: Tabley House façade as engraved for *Vitruvius Britannicus*. The turrets on the side wings were not executed.

Left: Tabley House, Cheshire. *Above:* Tabley House Stables.

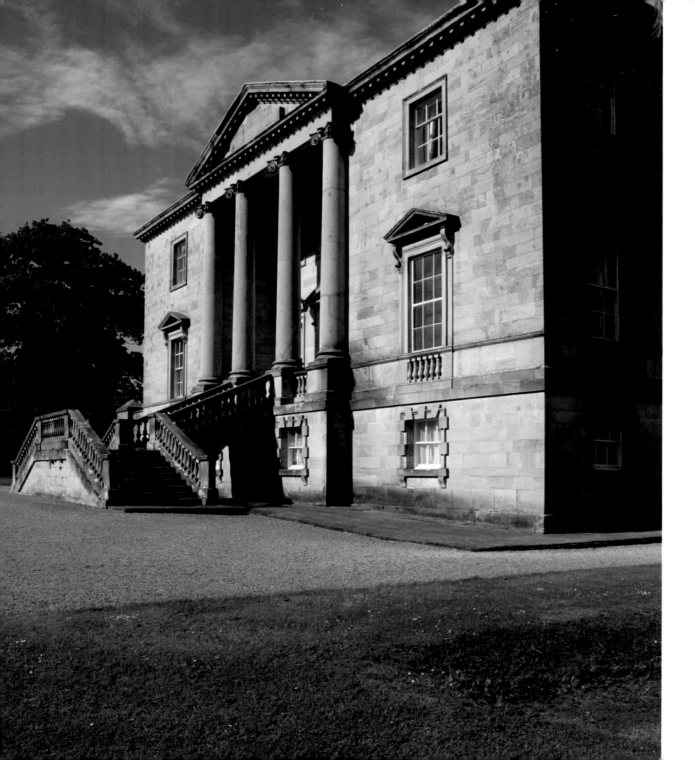

Country Houses:

Constable Burton Hall

The new house was built upon the site of the older Elizabethan mansion in order to take advantage of both the dramatic natural landscape, and the existing radiating lime avenues. The former suggested that a conventional Palladian villa with wings would not fit comfortably on the site, and so Carr determined that the tall main block would have the best outlook, and the domestic quarters and stables would be built as a low-built detached group to the north. The idea was exceptional at the time, and Carr cautiously did not reveal it in the engraving of the house in Vitruvius Britannicus.

As an economy measure it was good practice at the time to re-use the raw materials created by the demolition of the old house. The masonry of north front and the domestic quarters suggest such a use, and within the adjacent walls there is certainly decorative classical masonry. There is too Elizabethan panelling in a room above the old kitchen. In the wider landscape, Carr added a Gothick touch to an eyecatcher that also served as a farm, while the existing main road was redirected away from the house. The sturdy entrance gates on the A684 were sited so as to present a diagonal glimpse of the new mansion.

Left: Constable Burton Hall, North Yorkshire.

Right: Constable Burton Hall,
North Yorkshire.

Everingham Hall was rebuilt to Carr's design on the site of its medieval predecessor. The new house was a rectangle with a principal front facing west. It is possible that the fairly recent plantations, and the rides cut through them, influenced the character of the respective fronts.

The walling was of locally produced brick, with enough of each variety being fired to provide sufficient bricks to last the current building season. The need for a careful economy is shown by the varied qualities of the brick types used for each facade. The three tiers of windows were enlivened by contrasting dressings of stone, while by the use of 'dripping eaves' he eliminated the more conventional guttering.

Right: Everingham Hall

Country Houses: Thirsk Hall

Thirsk Hall in North Yorkshire is, like Fangfoss Hall, a close neighbour to its church. In 1771 Ralph Bell called in Carr to extend the existing Hall by placing a Great Room in the new north wing, with a stucco ceiling by James Henderson (duplicating that for Sir James Pennyman in Lairgate Hall, Beverley). There is a counterbalancing wing to the south. Carr also updated the entrance door, giving it a pediment on carved scrolling brackets. The house is still the residence of the Bell family.

Above & right: Thirsk Hall, N. Yorkshire.

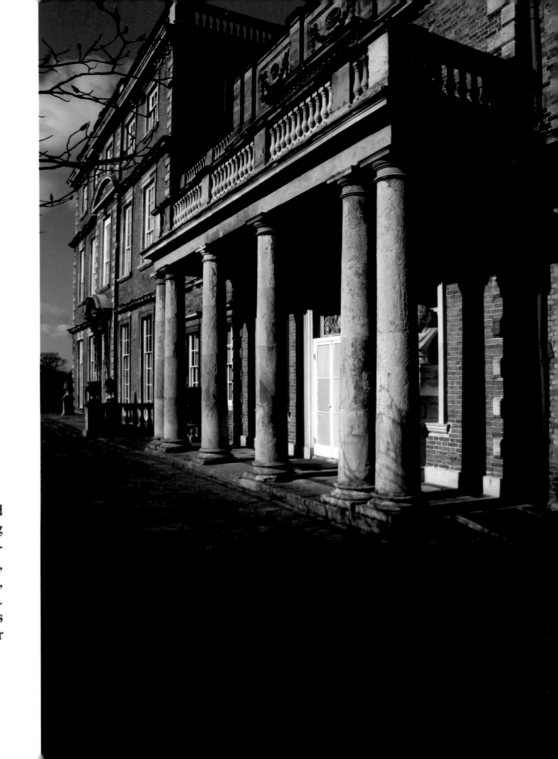

Newby Hall has a complex architectural history. Carr was called in to create an eastward extension in the form of two projecting much lower wings, the northern one to house the domestic quarters. The outcome was that within the shell of the southern one, Robert Adam created a brilliantly inventive Sculpture Gallery, which could be entered through Carr's six columned Doric porch. To mask his dome, Adam added the carved masonry above Carr's centrepiece while William Belwood subsequently made further additions over Carr's side elements.

Right: Newby Hall, Ripon, North Yorkshire.

Knaresborough House was designed for James Collins in a similar vein, with a taller centre flanked by a pair of much lower wings, a design Carr duplicated for the Waterhouse family at Well Head on the outskirts of Halifax. In both cases enrichment was confined to the Doric porches with their fluted friezes. Internally, William Peckitt designed and made the panels of stained glass in 1768, now in the staircase window.

Above left: Knaresborough House, North Yorkshire.

Fangfoss Hall was rebuilt by the Overend family circa 1760, just to the north of its church. The entrance and garden fronts are identical save for their respective porches: the former is Doric, the latter Ionic. The model is an engraving in Abraham Swan's "A Collection of Designs in Architecture of 1757". There was a short-lived vogue for pyramid roofs in the middle of the eighteenth century, and Carr had recently completed another one in the High Street of Northallerton. The front porch at Fangfoss was intended as a shelter from the rain whilst someone came to open the door, a practical touch Carr repeated elsewhere. The interiors are generously proportioned but they were detailed with an eye to economy. Thus the iron balustrade is plain, though with an iron twist to every third baluster.

Above right: Fangfoss Hall, East Yorkshire.

Fairfax House was built by the last Viscount Fairfax for the express purpose of attracting an appropriate Catholic suitor for Lady Anne, his only child and sole heiress. Previous suitors had included Thomas Clifton of Lytham Hall in Lancashire and William Constable of Burton Constable Hall in East Yorkshire. Both men were patrons of John Carr. It has been suggested that Lord Fairfax took over an incomplete shell, and that Carr was brought in to provide the internal finishings, much as he had recently done at nearby Kirby Hall. The circumstances offered a rare opportunity for an architectural display, much as one might find in London. On the principal floors every room has its complement of richly carved woodwork equal to the lavish stuccowork of the ceilings.

There were three hierarchies of expenditure: the reception rooms, the bedrooms and the attics, then the fireplaces and doorcases and then ceilings, whether painted or gilded. By such means the Georgian visitor would know exactly where he was standing.

Fairfax House was decorated during those few years when the Rococo style had just started to wane, but before the style we know as Neo-Classical had had time to settle down. So while there is nothing overtly Ancient Greek, there is much influence derived from the decorative detailing of Ancient Rome. Indeed a figure of Roma can be seen on the walls of the Staircase Hall, while the adjacent ceiling of the landing was based upon a fragment from the Temple of Venus and Rome on the Palatine Hill in Rome. Carr would find the motif among the published engravings of Andrea Palladio. There is too a link with Lytham Hall, whose marble chimneypiece in the Drawing Room is duplicated by that in the Library at Fairfax House.

The earlier Palladian style had had its ceilings divided into heavily framed compartments. Its successor experimented with a more complex geometry based upon ovals, or part ovals resembling C-Scrolls. The Neo-Classical returned to the rigid geometry of squares, octagons, diamonds and circles but favouring lighter compartments. All three modes can be found at Fairfax House.

Left: Fairfax House, York.

Above left: Carved wood Neo-Classical doorhead with a rope-like guilloche ornament. *Above right:* Carved wood Rococo doorhead using C-Scrolls. *Below left:* The Neo-Classical ceiling on the underside of the main staircase, based upon a Roman model. *Below right:* The Rococo ceiling of the Saloon with its oval framework *(All Fairfax House).*

Carr employed both English and foreign craftsmen. For carved wood the men were generally from Yorkshire, but much of his earlier stucco work was done by Italian speaking Swiss such as Giuseppe Cortese. The Continental manner can be seen in the Staircase Hall at Lytham, where the striking boldness of an upper cartouche contrasts with its counterpart below. In both woodwork and marble carving the most obvious Rococo motifs are the C-Scrolls. In the 'Adam' or Neo-Classical style that followed, craftsmen might mingle traditional woodcarving and the newly introduced 'Composition' especially for chimneypieces such as those at Clifton House Museum, where the influence of Wedgwood is clear.

Somerset House, Halifax, West Yorkshire, once stood at the edge of the town, hence the former large garden to the rear. The former prolonged facade once housed the Royds' family town mansion, their informal banking parlour and a complex range of warehouses. These were designed to hold bales of woollen cloth prior to their dispersal to both home and export markets.

The centrepiece contains a Great Room, which could occasionally serve such quasi-civic purposes as entertaining King Christian VII of Denmark in 1768. The former eastern section has been demolished, as has most of the interior, but the Great Room survives, together with one of the carved wooden chimneypieces whose

centre tablet depicts one of Aesop's fables; 'Take what you want but pay for it'.

Left: Somerset House, Halifax, West Yorkshire *(undergoing restoration). Above:* Somerset House Great Room.

Haggersgate House, Whitby, is here attributed to Carr. It was built circa 1760 for the Yeoman family, and is one of a small early group that are stylistically linked together: Fairfax House York, Everingham Hall, Everingham and Lytham Hall, Lytham St Annes. The house has a broad but very shallow site, and for a time at least it stood head and shoulders above its neighbours. It is probable that for a modest fee Carr provided little more than a plan and front elevation. In a town built largely out of local stone, the choice of a bright red brick with stone dressings must have seemed startling. Though all four houses differ in their sizes and secondary detailing, there remains a kinship.

Right: Haggersgate House, Whitby, North Yorkshire.

Town Houses: Clifton House

Clifton House, Rotherham, South Yorkshire, was one of the two suburban villas designed by Carr for members of the Walker family, the town's leading iron founders. Clifton was for Joshua (the now demolished Eastwood was for his brother Joseph). The principal rooms were not on the entrance front, but on the side and back of the house. The central core contains the clearstoried staircase hall. The house is a museum and has been since the 1890s. The interior is remarkably well preserved, and has an excellent sequence of 'composition' ornamented chimneypieces and overdoors.

Right: The Entrance front, Clifton House, Rotherham, built for Joshua Walker, 1783.

Below left: Detail of the Ionic Order of the Dining Room chimneypiece. Executed in carved wood and the fashionable manufactured product, 'composition'. The overflowing bowl of fruit reflects the use of the room, while the honeysuckle frieze duplicates one in the Crescent at Buxton.

Below centre: The small room on the left of the Entrance Hall gains presence by the use of simple shallow arches flanking the chimney breast, a device also used by Sir John Soane.

Below right: Carr's characteristic Roman-style vaulted Staircase Hall. The blue painted ironwork is typical of the Georgian period.

Buxton Crescent. Buxton, Derbyshire, with its warm waters, had been exploited by the Romans but, in the 18th century, the available accommodation was at the top of the hill, while the waters remained at the bottom. The Duke of Devonshire, with Carr's help, began to consider the creation of a new all-inclusive resort and spa, whose outcome included a revitalised baths, new pump room, boarding houses and hotels, a Great Stables, an Assembly Room, shops, scenic drives and promenades. It was to be financed through a copper mining windfall. From whichever way it is viewed, the Crescent is the dominant element, with its clean cut lines and meticulous attention to the detailing of each of the successive facades. In this it differs from the Royal Crescent at Bath. Only the tall arched windows of the Assembly Room break the general uniformity. Even the seven main chimneystacks are clustered into cruciform groups punctuating the skyline. The pilastered façade was inspired by Inigo Jones' Piazzas in Covent Garden, though with more correctly Neo-Classical detail. All access was via the arcading of the ground floor to reduce the impact of the harsher weather of the Pennines. This integration of all the necessary facilities was a novelty at the time, but one perhaps prompted by Carr's own month long visit in April 1775 when he took the waters 'in which I Bathe once a day'. Ten days later he reported that he 'crawls about with the help of a stick'. The subdivisions of the outline plan of the Crescent were based upon those of a Roman Theatre, while the vaulted vestibules to the lodging houses served also, in the Continental fashion, as vestibules to the shops. The kitchens were in the basement, and the servants slept within the

roof space. To reduce the risk of fire, the staircases were of stone, with elegant iron balustrades. The different classes of guests were carefully segregated, those that were first class faced south, the remainder, north. The Assembly Room was Carr's pièce de résistance, and despite its chequered career, it has managed to retain its original chandeliers.

The scale of the new development and its comparative isolation prompted the creation of a Great Stables on the slope north of the river and the Crescent. This is externally an irregular octagon of four longer and four much shorter sides, clothed overall with Carr's characteristic blind arcading whose blandness intentionally masks the drama of its circular colonnade of Doric columns each 28 feet high. In 1796 the visiting Carr family declared that this 'is the finest thing in Europe', but a contemporary detractor such as the Hon. John Byng, had claimed in 1790 that 'my Cavalry…are lodged in a most ill contrived, magnificent mews' (which possessed) 'useless, ill contrived grandeurs, but the Duke, I suppose was made prey of by some architect, a contrast of his Grace as having some genius and no fortune!'.

The arrival of the railways made the Great Stables redundant, but the seventh Duke was persuaded to allow the building to be converted into a hospital, and to be covered by a huge dome of iron and slate designed by Robert Rippon Duke. (Taken together, the work of Carr and Duke surely influenced the interior of Vincent Harris's Manchester Central Reference Library of the 1930s). In turn, the Devonshire Royal Hospital vacated the building, and it now serves as a department of the University of Derby.

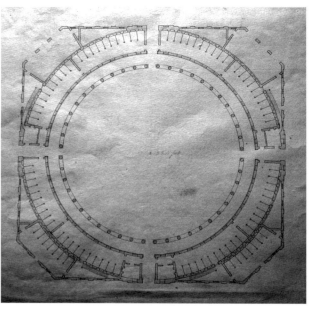

Above: An early plan of the stables at Buxton. The stalls are arranged in a circular fashion.

Above: Buxton Crescent, top left and the domed Great Stables, middle right, set adjacent to parkland. *(Jason Hawkes Aerial Photography)*

Above: The Crescent at Buxton, Derbyshire.

Carr was essentially self-educated, firstly as a practicing stonemason, and then in the many branches of the quite separate art of architecture. What are its rules and when should one break them? What are the tenets of Classical Architecture, and should they be applied to other styles? What are the respective roles of proportion and decoration? How far should an architect take a client into his confidence? These and many other questions will arise once the design process has begun. In effect the architect is doing a tricky diplomatic balancing act throughout.

Architects from the age of James Gibbs (1684-1754) onward recognised that in the fiercely competitive fields of contemporary architecture and furniture making, skilful publicity was an essential. Successful self-publicity, making the necessary designs, and securing the right engravers was personally time consuming, and highly expensive, while in the case of style, timing was all important. Adam failed fully to publish in his lifetime, Chambers only completed his first volume, and neither Sheraton nor Hepplewhite, though achieving widespread publicity, can be shown to have produced any furniture themselves, such is the power of self advertisement. John Carr and James Wyatt devoted themselves to architectural practice rather than publishing and publicity, but in consequence their actual output has remained comparatively obscure, despite the fact that they were undoubtedly the most prolific architects of their generation.

Carr's contribution to eighteenth century architecture rests upon the exceptional variety of building types he designed, and the care he took with their planning and detailing. He tried to minimise the waste spaces typically associated with passages and corridors, while trying to make them visually interesting to their day-to-day users. This led to the development of top-lit centrally planned staircase halls. Indeed, like James Wyatt, he took much interest in staircase design and construction, using iron to reinforce their structural strength. The staircase was also used as a vehicle to give easier access in those older houses where the floor plates were at different levels.

In his disposition of the rooms round the central core, Carr often placed inward-looking rooms such as dining rooms, music rooms and libraries facing north. Drawing rooms and saloons could face south, to balance the outward views toward the landscape on the one hand, and the conversation on the other, while bedrooms might comfortably face east toward the morning sun. The canted bay windows served the dual purpose of providing 'movement' to the exterior, as at Constable Burton, and an excellent vantage point for viewing the landscape from the interior. Indeed he sometimes went further and positioned a fireplace beneath its middle window sill to enjoy both the view, and the fire at the same time. There are such at both Tabley House and Heath Hall. Within these characteristic bay windows, the rooms might be octagonal, circular, oval, or with an apse at one end or both. Adam is often cited for the variety of his room shapes, but Carr was no less adept.

Where there was a greater perceived risk of fire, as in the new hotels in Buxton, the steps were of stone with iron balustrades, and malleable cast-iron was preferred to the use of wood for those window sills in the Crescent at Buxton which would be difficult to inspect and repair once the builders' scaffolding had been taken down. Indeed the Crescent is a model of careful design and detailing, and thus unsurprisingly was chosen by Carr to represent his work on his formal portrait by Sir William Beechey.

As regards his numerous public bridges, he took the view that the rapid rise in the prosperity of the area within his Surveyorship would outpace the capital expenditure upon them, unless all new work exceeded the currently required capacity. He managed to get his employers to agree with this forecast, and as a result much if not all of his new work is still (but only just) adequate in its width to take current levels of traffic. He was also astute enough to recognise that as the roads improved, traffic speeds would increase and as one consequence the gradients, sight lines and turning circles would have to be redesigned to take account of these new factors. It appears to be the case that not one of Carr's bridges has subsequently collapsed, which is more than can be claimed for most of his significant contemporaries.

The selection of illustrations in this book has been partly guided by accessibility to the public and partly because they are representative of his style during his very long working lifetime.

Newark had a long history as a prosperous Nottinghamshire borough on the Great North Road, and was one of the latter's major stopping places. By the 1770s the Corporation and its aristocratic backers decided to provide a new civic building worthy of Newark's social and political status, and in 1773 Carr successfully competed against London men to win the commission. He, like Paine at Doncaster, decided to incorporate two elegant houses into the scheme whose rents would go to support the remainder, but Carr learnt from Paine that the house fronts must be fully integrated into the whole façade, and their sites be of much more modest dimensions if they were to succeed. The plan would have to be multifunctional, and its elements separable for security purposes.

In the front part of the ground floor, space was allotted to a cornmarket; behind that there was a much larger pillared butter market, and beyond that a courtyard given over to the fixed stalls of a butchers' shambles.

On the first floor, in addition to the loggia overlooking the Market Place, there was to be a room for corporation business, then a principal staircase whose landing also served the Assembly Room for dancing and concerts. One of the adjacent smaller rooms could be used as a Card Room, another to house the temporary furniture required when the Assembly Room was needed as a Court Room at Quarter Sessions, or for the storage of a theatre or concert stage, and any temporary scenery. The new Town Hall at Newark was thus an early example of a multi-purpose Civic Centre.

Right: Newark Town Hall Assembly Room interior.

Left page: Newark Town Hall, Newark-on-Trent, Nottinghamshire.

Lodges and Gateways

The rising social tensions which were to culminate in the French Revolution, prompted many landowners to consider the better protection of their houses and parks, and the park wall and its gateways and lodges represent one overt reaction. Another was the diversion of public roads away from the mansion house, though some considered it to be desirable to allow a distant glimpse of the house between the piers of a carefully sited gateway. From the 1770s onwards, many were tempted to substitute a manned lodge for an unmanned gateway. Thus within thirty years Harewood was to have Carr's Lofthouse Gates, Robert Adam's Porter's Lodge, and Carr's Grand Lodge.

The initial designs for the Grand Lodge, in Harewood village, West Yorkshire, were by Humphry Repton, and were intended to be the climax of the vista along The Avenue. Lord Harewood at first encouraged Repton, but later changed his mind in favour of Carr whose designs incorporated the residential parts of Adam's Porter's Lodge as outliers to the much grander Roman Triumphal Arch proposed by Carr. Repton was furious but could do nothing except utter veiled but futile condemnation of his rival. The Lodge comprises two three-storey houses linked by an arch, i.e. they have their kitchens in the basement like a London town house. All that is left of Repton's scheme is the symmetrical widening of the end of The Avenue. The internal design of the arch is worthy of notice.

Previous page: Fillingham Castle Lodge, Lincolnshire.
Next page: Harewood Grand Lodge, each half a three storey house *(by kind permission of the Earl and Countess of Harewood).*

Below left: Arch of Septimus Severus, Rome, 17th Century engraving and a Roman model for the Grand Lodge. *Middle:* Ormesby Hall Lodges, Cleveland. *Right:* Harewood Grand Lodge interior of arch.

Stables: Castle Howard

The stable fronts at Castle Howard and Raven-field are based upon a three-fold repetition of a simplified Roman triumphal arch. The stables at Castle Howard date from the 1770s, and were financed by the fifth Earl of Carlisle out of the sale of estate timber including the twigs, which were sold in bundles for broom making.

Carr gained the commission after the designs of Sir William Chambers were rejected as too

expensive, but he tactfully placed a rectangular Chambersian attic above the columns of the centrepiece. The main walling was built up out of courses of diminishing height so as to enhance the perspective effect, and the overall costs were reduced by paring down accommodation above the ground floor. One unusual feature is the pebble mosaic paved carpet within the courtyard.

Carr's building is the first to greet the visitor to Castle Howard, which lies some distance beyond, and it concluded the daunting architectural programme that had been initiated by the third Earl in 1700.

Above: The stables at Castle Howard, North Yorkshire.

The stables at Ravenfield are an early example of Carr's use of the Roman triumphal arch motif. The block stands at the south end of a significant row of Carr's farm buildings, now all converted into housing.

Above: The stables at Ravenfield Hall, South Yorkshire.

Santo Antonio Hospital. The intended hospital of Santo Antonio at Oporto in Portugal was on a truly palatial scale, equal in size to the Vieux Cour of the Louvre. Oporto was, and remains, Portugal's second city, and a leader in both the manufacture and export of wine. In its turn, Georgian York was an important centre of the wine trade, and its leading families lived close to the city. It was families such as the Thompsons, (of Kirby Hall) and the Crofts, who secured this plum commission for Carr. He charged a fee of £500 for his designs, but accepted that it would be built and supervised by the Portuguese. The plans set sail from Hull in 1769. Though Carr was badly advised about the proposed site, whose contours were wholly unsuited to a quadrangular plan, the charity went ahead regardless, and sadly only one third had achieved completion by the early nineteenth century. Every department from the maternity wards to the mortuary was allotted a place, and less usually, so too were the mentally ill and the incurable. Roof water was collected in tanks to service more than 200 water closets adjacent to both wards and kitchens. The corridors doubled as places for convalescents to exercise, and balconies were directly accessible from the wards, for the sick to gain fresh air. The first patients moved in at the turn of the eighteenth century.

Above: Santo Antonio Hospital, Oporto, Portugal.

Bootham Park Hospital, York. The ample site provides a convincingly park-like setting, and the initial impression is indeed that of a handsome country mansion. Nor do the red brick and stone dressings suggest otherwise. The centrepiece is an engaged Doric portico, with, until fairly recently, a domed Doric cupola rising from the roof. The 'piano nobile' has blind arcading whose variations are a subtlety of invention. Only the heavy rustication of the entrance doorcase offers hints at a public rather than a private function. The end elevations are notable for their asymmetry, in part perhaps because additional wings had been proposed.

Right: Bootham Park Hospital, York. *Below:* Bootham Park Hospital, end elevation.

John Webb (1611-72) was perhaps the first English architect to design a 'model farm', but the type swept through England and Scotland during the eighteenth and nineteenth centuries. The farmhouse was the natural centrepiece, flanked by accommodation for both animals and crops, but occasionally Carr incorporated farm buildings within a 'square of stables'. Each farming family now lived in splendid isolation, but was often cut off from a direct participation in village life.

Campsmount Home Farm, Campsall, South Yorkshire, was an extensive complex built, together with the new Hall, for Thomas Yarborough circa 1752. The individual components were symmetrical, though their arrangement was not. The overall style was that of Lord Burlington, i.e. Palladian. The barn ventilation included the Gothick arrow slits Carr had seen in the York city walls.

The Plompton Hall Estate Farms, near Knaresborough, North Yorkshire, date from the later 1750s, and were built for Daniel Lascelles the younger brother of Edwin Lascelles of Harewood House. Unusually they antedate the rebuilding of the Hall, and were on a scale to cause financial difficulties. The long drawn out elevation of Plompton Grange Farm originally had consistently Gothick detailing, later much modified. To its north east, Carr built Loxley Farm, a near duplicate of Round Hill Farm on the Hornby Castle Estate. To the west Carr designed the Home Farm which, with its numerous appendages, was closely integrated with the Stable Court, one wing of which is an early example of a Barn conversion. The latter was then renamed Plompton Hall. The Home Farm House itself is an exercise in solid geometry and in a style reminiscent of Sir John Vanbrugh. The long range of nearby 'hovels' are characteristically Carr, and display his careful attention to roof construction. The group of farms on the Hornby Castle Estate in North Yorkshire were built for the last Earl of Holderness in the mid 1760s. Arbour Hill Farm and its twin Street House Farm served the dual purpose of farm and 'eyecatcher'. The former is of stone and its silhouette was to be viewed from the windows of Hornby Castle, the latter is of brick and still catches the eye of travellers along the Great North Road. The composition of the front has its five parts symmetrically arranged in the Palladian manner, but when seen from the end, its forms overlap into an arrangement wholly picturesque.

Byram Hall was extensively enlarged for Sir John Ramsden from the mid eighteenth century onward. Its Home Farm comprised a great open court with the Farm House in the middle of one side and an exceptionally long range of barns on the other. The two ranges were flanked by the colonnades of the animal shelters. The whole composition recalls the sketchy paintings of Ancient Roman seaside villas, then newly excavated. The building material here is a coarse rubble, rendered and colourwashed. Behind the Barn range is a row of cart sheds constructed of ashlar.

Below left: Byram Park Home Farm, West Yorkshire. *Below right:* Roundhill Farm, North Yorkshire.

Top left: Plompton Grange Farm, North Yorkshire, a Gothick eyecatcher. *Middle top:* Norton Hall Stables, South Yorkshire. *Top right:* Campsmount Home Farm, Campsall, South Yorkshire. *Below:* Arbour Hill Farm, Hornby, North Yorkshire.

Above: Appersett Bridge, North Yorkshire. A former packhorse bridge, which was widened in 1795 to take carts and carriages nearer to the Lake District. The widening also involved the construction of a by-pass round the back of the village, to obviate the demolition of existing properties.

Right: Rutherford Bridge North Yorkshire, wholly rebuilt following the great flood of 1771. The original bridge had two arches, replaced by this, Carr's greatest span.

Previous page: Blyth Bridge, Blyth, Nottinghamshire.

Above: Croft Bridge, North Yorkshire, was acknowledged by Carr to be a fine medieval structure, probably dating from the fourteenth century. It once formed a crossing of the River Tees as part of the Great North Road. Carr largely replicated the earlier work, though his new cornice was of decidedly Roman inspiration.

Right: Downholme Bridge, North Yorkshire, a new bridge (cost £1,200) following the storm of 1771 . Its three arches are of widely varying span and support a quite steeply inclined road. Carr carefully avoided drawing attention to this design problem by treating the elevations with total simplicity. The bridge has a background of wooded cliffs and a rocky escarpment, and it

achieves a fitting simplicity of design. *(Photograph D. Foster).*

Above: Reeth Bridge, North Yorkshire, has sharply angular elevations that contrast with the flatness of its setting. The overall feeling shows a subtle understanding of medieval design unusual for a date of the 1770s.

Right: Masham Bridge, North Yorkshire, is dated 1754, and its profiles are modelled upon those of the Ponte Sant'Angelo in Rome. Their pier fronts approximate to a catenary curve but in the Roman example this profile is confined to the upstream elevation. The aim was to reduce the impact of floodwater on the sides of the piers, instead directing the flow toward the centre of the waterway. This insistence upon a smoother flow, led to the curved surfaces of other elements of the bridge. The bridge is publicly attributed to Carr's father Robert Carr but at that time father and son were also in an informal partnership. Masham Bridge was widened circa 1908.

Above: Ferrybridge Bridge, South Yorkshire, was a replacement for two earlier bridges, but though Carr was no longer a joint bridgemaster to the West Riding, the Magistrates decided nevertheless to ask him to enter the competition for the new project. Building lasted from 1797 to 1804. Carr added a Toll House at one end of the bridge. His earlier pierfronts had been either flat pilasters or semicircular ones, but here they were to be boldly half octagons given an overall pattern of rustication, while the balustrade was designed to be vandal-proof.

Right: Otterington Bridge, North Yorkshire, a deceptively simple bridge of 1776, again in the Ancient Roman manner. It has the air of a feature inset into a gentleman's landscaped park.

Above: Catterick Bridge, North Yorkshire, partially dates from the fifteenth century and was widened by Carr in 1792 (cost £2980) to take the increasing volumes of traffic using the Great North Road. In principle, Carr followed the medieval work, though with much altered detail.

Above: Crambeck Bridge on the York to Malton Turnpike. It was economically built of rubble, to be covered with a coating of render. The flat roadway is supported by a sequence of ten arches in imitation of the austerity of ancient Roman aqueducts or viaducts, but also anticipating the railway viaducts that became a commonplace throughout much of the nineteenth century.

Insert: Ribblehead Railway Viaduct, North Yorkshire, 1875

Bridges

John Carr's bridge-building career was started when the Magistrates for the West Riding sought professional advice from their two County Surveyors, of whom one was John Carr's father Robert Carr (1697-1760), a practicing stonemason and building contractor. John Carr succeeded his father in 1760, but resigned the West Riding post in 1772, to take up a sole Surveyorship in the North Riding, for whom he went on to design the majority of his bridges.

The duties of the Surveyor included a responsibility for the maintenance and design all the county's buildings, and specifically the conduct of an annual survey of all the county's bridges. In 1752, the West Riding County Magistrates commissioned Robert Carr to prepare a Bridge Book containing an elevation and plan of each county bridge in order to forestall attempts to pass off a bridge as a property of the county. Since many of the resultant drawings are signed J.C. it is presumed that the survey was a joint work of the father and his son. Its preparation gave John Carr a unique opportunity to travel throughout the county, and to get to know something of its varied topography, geology, and the manner in which the stonemasons of each locality had developed a style to suit the needs and raw materials of their area.

Carr's great chance occurred when a huge rainstorm devastated much of the North East in November 1771, necessitating either the restoration or the complete rebuilding of many bridges, a renewal which, once completed, also made clear how many of the surviving bridges had become inadequate for the increasing traffic generated by Yorkshire's trade and industry. Carr was farseeing enough to realise that since this increase would lead to a demand for further improvement, it made sense to address the task now rather than more expensively later. (Here he differed from contemporary Yorkshire bridge builders such as the Gott family). As a result most, though not all, of Carr's bridges have retained their original widths. A few such as Masham Bridge, North Yorkshire (1754) have been doubled in width, while the bridges at Crambeck and Ayton each have a new bridge built alongside.

With a handful of exceptions, Carr's consistent policy was to build well, with a most careful attention to economy, but when sufficient money was available a little ornament might be placed on the side most clearly in public view. Conversely, the more decorative elevations of Blyth Bridge and Greta Bridge faced on to the respective landscaped parks of the Mellishes and the Morritts who were obliged to pay for the additional ornament. The bridge at Ferrybridge, West Yorkshire, 1797 (River Aire) is the only publicly-financed one to have a decorative balustrade, which was inset into the exterior of the parapet to minimise the risk of vandalism. Even then his sense of economy was brought into play, for it was cheaper to turn a full baluster on a lathe, than conventionally to carve half of one on to a larger block of stone. Another unconventional practice was to group his balusters into even rather than odd numbers.

The architectural style adopted by Carr was based upon Antique Roman precedent e.g. Crambeck, but, with one notable exception, his preference was for the segmental arch, (a medieval development), rather than the standard semicircular arch adopted by the Romans. He avoided the use of the then fashionable alternative, the semi-elliptical arch, though one can be found at the bridges in the park of Harewood House and at Coniston Cold.

Churches: Boynton Church

Far more churches were built or enlarged during the Georgian era than commentators are generally willing to allow, in part because of the intense Victorian dislike of a style they deemed irremediably pagan in origin. Sadly none of Carr's churches has survived without Victorian meddling. His church work divides neatly into existing churches in need of repair and which were the financial responsibility of the parish, and new churches built at the cost of private patrons. Unsurprisingly some wanted to retain at least a semblance of the Gothic, for example the largely rebuilt parish church at Boynton, or the new private chapel at Denton. The plan of Boynton is unusual for there is a quartet of columns in the centre enclosing the chancel, beyond which is a mortuary chapel housing the monuments to the Boynton family. The western end is taken up by the gallery, which spans the stairs and the vestry beneath.

Left and above: Boynton Church, East Yorkshire.

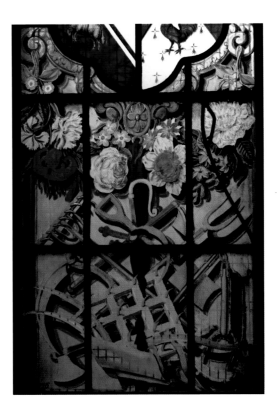

Denton Chapel was built as a replacement to the family chapel near the site of the former Denton Hall, a seat of the Fairfaxes and latterly of the Ibbetsons. Sir James Ibbetson salvaged the early eighteenth century glass depicting King David and a contemporary armorial panel both by Henry Gyles of York. Sir James had the smaller panel supplemented by one signed by William Peckitt also of York. The upper part is again armorial beneath which is a rococo composition of flowers and agricultural implements. The enclosing masonry takes the form of a Gothick Venetian window. The classical font is larger than one might expect for a chapel suggesting it might come from elsewhere.

Left and above: Denton Church, North Yorkshire.

St Peter and St Leonard's Horbury. The old chapel of ease was a part of the ancient parish of Wakefield, but had become too small and dilapidated to serve a growing and more prosperous local population. Carr generously decided to rebuild on a new and more splendid scale, entirely at his own expense, between 1791 and 1794. The greatest subsequent change has been the removal of the pairs of Corinthian columns in front of the altar space, and the organ gallery.

Previous page & above: York Minster stained glass by William Peckitt; part of a refurbishment by Carr that included the Chapter House ceiling on the next page.

Left: Garden Temple, Kilnwick Hall, East Yorkshire, one of the few surviving drawings by Carr. *Middle:* Plompton Hall showing textured wall surface. *Right:* Obelisk, Bramham Park, West Yorkshire, (*D. Foster*).

Below: left to right: The Orders: Ionic at Fangfoss Hall, Corinthian at Lytham Hall and Tuscan at Harewood House, *(by kind permission of the Earl and Countess of Harewood).*

Selected List of Works

BRIDGES

North Riding of Yorkshire
Appersett, 1795
Aysgarth, 1788
Ayton, 1775
Bainbridge(Yore Bridge), 1793
Bow Bridge, 1789
Catterick, 1792
Crambeck 1785
Croft, 1795,
Danby Wiske, 1782
Downholme, 1773
Greta Bridge, 1773
Grinton, 1797
Hawnby, 1800
Low Bourne, 1775
Morton on Swale, 1800
Otterington, 1776
Reeth, 1772-3
Riccal, 1803
Richmond, 1789
Rutherford, 1773
Skipton on Swale, 1781
Strensall, 1798
Thirsk Mill Bridge, 1789
Yarm, 1806-10
West Riding of Yorkshire
Carlton Ferry, (partially standing), 1774
Coniston Cold, 1763
Skip Bridge, 1787
Harewood Park Bridge (private), 1771

CHURCHES

Bierley, Bradford, 1766
Boynton, 1768-70
Denton, nr. Otley, 1776
Dewsbury, partial reconstruction, 1765-7
Horbury, Wakefield, 1791-3
Ossington, 1782-3
Ravenfield, 1756
Rokeby, completed 1777-8
Sheffield St.Peter, repairs and alterations, 1773-5
York Minster restorations, 1770-3 and 1794-7

COUNTRY HOUSES AND / OR THEIR ESTATE BUILDINGS

Alderton Rectory, 1772
Arncliffe Hall, 1750-54
Arthington Hall, 1760-70
Aske Hall, c. 1765
Aston Hall, 1767-72
Aston Rectory, 1770
Auckland Castle, 1767-73
Basildon Park, 1776-83
Belle Isle, c.1795
Belle Vue, Hawkeshead, c.1799
Blyth Hall and bridge, 1773-6
Bolling Hall, 1779-80
Boynton Hall, 1765-80
Bramham Park, obelisk, after 1763
Bretton Hall, 1793
Byram Park Home Farm & Stables, 1760
Cannon Hall, 1764-7
Castle Farm, Sledmere Hall, 1778
Castle Howard Stables, 1774-82
Castle William, c.1789
Chatsworth House, internal remodelling, 1782-84
Chesters, 1771
Clifton Hall Nottingham, 1778-97
Clifton House, Rotherham, 1783
Clints Hall (Richmond), 1762-3
Colwick Hall, 1776
Constable Burton Hall, 1762-67
Coolattin, 1800-08
Courteenhall Stables, after 1763
Denton Park, 1772-8
Durham Castle, gateway, 1791
Ellenthorpe Hall, c.1777
Escrick Park, 1763-5
Everingham Hall, 1758-64
Farnley Hall, Otley, 1786-90
Fawley Court Lodges, 1797-8
Fixby Hall, c.1780
Gilling Castle, 1755-6
Gledhow Hall, 1766-7
Gledstone Hall, c.1772
Goldsborough Hall, 1764-5
Grimston Garth, 1781-86
Grove Hall, Darrington, (gateway), c.1783

Hardwick Hall, Derbyshire, extensive restoration, 1785-91
Harewood House, 1755-71
Hawksworth Hall, 1774
Heath Hall, 1754-80
Holker Hall, c.1783
Hornby Castle, 1760-70
Huthwaite Hall, 1748
Kirby Hall, 1747-55
Kirkland Hall, 1760
Kirkleatham Hall, 1764-7
Kirklees Hall, 1759-60
Knaresborough House, 1768
Lairgate Hall, Beverley, c.1773
Leventhorpe Hall, 1774
Lytham Hall, 1757-64
Middleton Lodge, 1777-80
Milton House, Peterborough, 1803
New Lodge, Barnsley, 1795
Newby Hall (Ripon), 1758-60
Norton Hall, Sheffield, 1768-9
Norton Place, 1776
Ormesby Hall, 1772
Panton Hall (fittings now at Basildon Park), 1775
Plompton Hall, 1755
Raby Castle, 1781 -5
Ravenfield Hall, 1760-78
Redbourne Hall gateway, 1773
Ribston Hall, c.1775
Rokeby Hall, c.1776
Sedbury Park estate buildings, c.1770
Stapleton Park, 1762-4
Staunton Hall, 1778-80
Swinton Park, 1764-7
Tabley House, 1760-67
Tankersley Park temple,
Thirsk Hall, 1771-3
Thornes House, Wakefield, 1779-81
Thorp Arch Hall, 1749-56
Towneley Hall, 1766-70
Welbeck Abbey, 1763
Wentworth Woodhouse, 1762-1804
White Windows, 1762-8
Wiganthorpe Hall (collection of drawings), c.1778

Winestead Stables, 1762
Wood Hall, Wetherby, c.1795
Workington Hall, 1783-91

PUBLIC BUILDINGS

The Assize Courts, 1773-7 and matching Female Prison, York, 1780-3
Bootham Park Hospital, York, 1774-77
Buxton Crescent, including the Assembly Rooms, 1779-90
Lincoln County Hospital, 1776-7
Newark Town Hall, including the Assembly Rooms, 1773-6
The Pikeing Well-House, New Walk, York, 1752-6
S. Antonio Hospital, Oporto, Portugal, begun 1770, halted 1845

TOWN HOUSES

Northallerton: Mitford House, High Street, c.1755
London: Royal Institution, Albemarle Street, c.1775
London: Burlington House, Piccadilly, of Carr's alterations of 1771-6, only a marble chimneypiece can now be seen.
Worksop: house in Potter Street, 1768-9,
York: 47, Bootham, 1752
Garforth House, Micklegate, 1754
Fairfax House, Castlegate, 1762-3
Castlegate House, Castlegate, 1762-3
Skeldergate House, Skeldergate, 1765-6 (Carr's own house, demolished).

A select list of buildings by John Carr, generally excluding buildings now demolished. The dates can sometimes be approximate. The list has been extracted from Sir Howard Colvin's 'Dictionary of British Architects' pp. 223-229.

Index

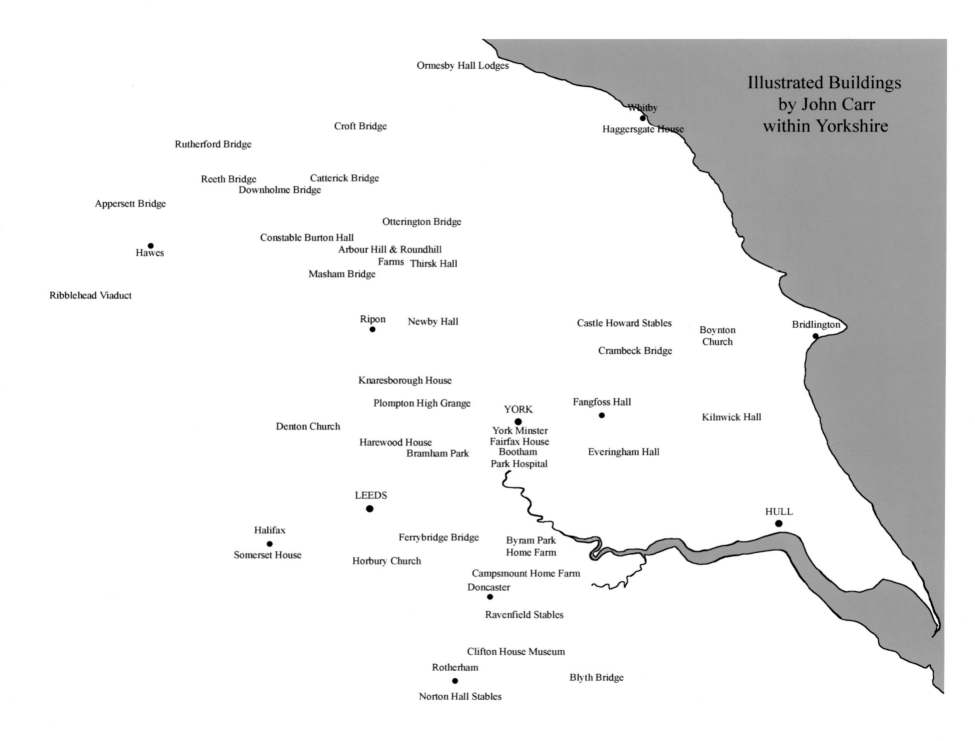

Illustrated Buildings
by John Carr
within Yorkshire

Ormesby Hall Lodges

Whitby

Haggersgate House

Croft Bridge

Rutherford Bridge

Reeth Bridge   Catterick Bridge
          Downholme Bridge

Appersett Bridge

                    Otterington Bridge

          Constable Burton Hall

                Arbour Hill & Roundhill
Hawes   Farms   Thirsk Hall

          Masham Bridge

Ribblehead Viaduct

                                        Castle Howard Stables
          Ripon   Newby Hall   Boynton
                                                               Church   Bridlington
                                          Crambeck Bridge

              Knaresborough House

              Plompton High Grange   YORK   Fangfoss Hall
                                                                      Kilnwick Hall
Denton Church
                                          York Minster
          Harewood House   Fairfax House
              Bramham Park   Bootham   Everingham Hall
                                          Park Hospital

          LEEDS
                                                                              HULL

Halifax   Ferrybridge Bridge   Byram Park
Somerset House   Home Farm
                    Horbury Church

                              Campsmount Home Farm
                              Doncaster

                              Ravenfield Stables

                    Clifton House Museum
          Rotherham
                              Blyth Bridge
          Norton Hall Stables